THE YALE DRAMA SERIES

David Charles Horn Foundation

The Yale Drama Series is funded by the generous support of the David Charles Horn Foundation, established in 2003 by Francine Horn to honor the memory of her husband, David. In keeping with David Horn's lifetime commitment to the written word, the David Charles Horn Foundation commemorates his aspirations and achievements by supporting new initiatives in the literary and dramatic arts.

Jar of Fat

SEAYOUNG YIM

Foreword by
Frances Ya-Chu Cowhig
Jacqueline Goldfinger
Virginia Grise
Rachel Lynett
Neil Wechsler
Leah Nanako Winkler

Yale UNIVERSITY PRESS/NEW HAVEN & LONDON

Yale University Press books may be purchased in quantity for educational,
business, or promotional use. For information, please e-mail
sales.press@yale.edu (U.S. office) or sales@yaleup.co.uk (U.K. office).

Set in ITC Galliard and Sabon types by Integrated Publishing Solutions.
Printed in the United States of America.

Library of Congress Control Number: 2022950327
ISBN 978-0-300-26801-0 (paperback : alk. paper)

A catalogue record for this book is available from the British Library.

This paper meets the requirements of ANSI/NISO Z39.48-1992
(Permanence of Paper).

10 9 8 7 6 5 4 3 2 1

For all the fat kids, with love

Beauty is, in some ways, boring. Even if its concept changes through the ages, nevertheless a beautiful object must always follow certain rules. . . . Ugliness is unpredictable and offers an infinite range of possibilities. Beauty is finite. Ugliness is infinite, like God.
   —Umberto Eco, *On Ugliness*

Contents

Foreword

For the first time in its fifteen-year history, the 2022 Yale Drama Series competition was adjudicated by a panel of judges, rather than by a single judge. This presented unique challenges, the first of which was to decide among ourselves how to manage the reading of more than 1,500 submissions from fifty-six countries. We, the six judges, are all former winners of the prize: Neil Wechsler (2008), Frances Ya-Chu Cowhig (2009), Virginia Grise (2010), Jacqueline Goldfinger (2017), Leah Nanako Winkler (2018), and Rachel Lynett (2021). Working alongside one additional reader, fellow playwright Susan Stanton, we divided the submissions into individual reading assignments of about 220 plays each in the fall of 2021, with the initial task of identifying the top 5 from our respective batches, to arrive at 35 finalists. We then each read all 35 finalists and generated new individual "top 5" lists from the finalists in preparation for a January Zoom-based convening, where, after several months of reading in isolation, we would discuss the finalists and determine the winner.

During the first half of our January meeting, we winnowed the thirty-five finalists to a shortlist of eight. We decided, in consultation with Yale Drama Series founder Francine Horn, to publicly recognize the entire shortlist, in hopes that showcasing these singular voices and visions would encourage producers to read their exciting new works, many of which were drafted amid the unprecedented shutdowns and social isolation of the pandemic.

The eight plays on our shortlist are: *All Eight*, by Lilly Camp, a fascinating exploration of the power dynamics of nine freshmen women on a college crew team; *Tell Me I'm Gorgeous at the End of the World*, by Aaron Coleman, a raw and wild piece about two queer men of color seeking a place in their community; *Midnight Showing*, by Libby Heily, a boldly theatrical play about the career of an uncompromising filmmaker; *A Medusa Thread*, by Candrice Jones, a poignant exploration of sexual assault and its aftermath from a uniquely Black perspective; *a home what howls (or the house what was ravine)*, by Matthew Paul Olmos, an epic piece about a Mexican American family trying to resist white real estate developers and evade eviction; *A Driving Beat*, by Jordan Ramirez Puckett, an unforgettable play about a mother and son forced to reconcile their different cultural heritages on a cross-country road trip; *The Jersey Devil Is a Papi Chulo*, by Iraisa Ann Reilly, a smart comedy about five American-Latina friends who encounter two white papi chulos (hotties) on a camping trip; and *Jar of Fat*, by Seayoung Yim, a wickedly funny, irreverent, and vicious satire on Korean beauty standards.

As we discussed the eight plays on our shortlist, one play kept rising to the top: *Jar of Fat*, by Seayoung Yim. Set in a fantastical fairy-tale world in which two Korean American sisters are deemed too fat to fit in their family grave, the play tackles some of the biggest taboos in both Korean and U.S. society—body weight and beauty standards—through a wonderfully specific cultural lens. The judge who first encountered *Jar of Fat* in the initial batch of plays found the script radical, honest, and searing. In a time when rage is not always allowed to women, especially not women of color, this judge found it incredible to come across a play that held so much rage while also not afraid to laugh at itself and the audience. It was like having a conversation with a playwright who remembered that theater is a playground and was daring her audience to play along.

Another judge was delighted to encounter in *Jar of Fat* a loud, unabashed voice writing about nonsubmissive Asian female characters in a funny, visceral, Artaudian way that crackled with both humor and pain in its treatment of body image issues that the judge felt were more typically reserved for white women. Yet another judge was drawn to the play's epic structure and vicious satirical voice.

As we continued to talk about *Jar of Fat*, we became intrigued by the questions opened up by the play: Can we simultaneously heal from and honor our traditions? How can we carry our stories forward while also healing from choices we made to survive? What does it mean to hold on to your culture and be critical of generational trauma without centering a Western view?

We loved that *Jar of Fat* doesn't shy away from going big in a world where smallness—especially for women—is celebrated, even in language. We found the play to be beautifully written, with surprising moments of humor, juxtaposed with piercing, brutal language.

For its audacity and singularity of vision, we chose Seayoung Yim's *Jar of Fat* as the winner of the 2022 Yale Drama Series prize. Yim's work is bold, unapologetic, hilarious, and shockingly modern. We recently had the privilege of speaking with her about her play and can think of no better way to close this Foreword and our collective work on the 2022 Yale Drama Series than with Seayoung's own words:

> *Jar of Fat* is a darkly comedic Korean American fairy tale about the allure and danger entangled within the quest for beauty and thinness. I grew up feeling like my shifting

weight was the top thing that people remarked about me. I have joked that I grew up with a standard of beauty that is fatless or dead. This became a seed for the play. What are the most extreme lengths a character could go to achieve a beauty and body that's nearly impossible to reach? What is the cost? What is the allure?

Like many children of immigrants, I have felt bewildered by having to adapt and adhere to multiple cultures which at times were at odds with each other. I wanted to look at those contradictions and clashes from a Korean American perspective. In my family, as well as in many other Asian American families, fat shaming is not taboo. It's often seen as a gesture of love and caring, of paying close attention, which adds a layer of complexity to the pain it causes. It is this infuriating enmeshment of familial love and harm that I wanted to explore in this play.

I have been obsessed with beauty standards and fat-phobia for some time. These are depressing and enraging obsessions that I'm sick of living with and want to explore using humor, which I find disarming and helpful for cracking open difficult topics.

I offer this play as a struck match to burn some of the accumulated rage at what anti-fat bias steals from us every day: grace, space, possibility, and breath. As a Korean American, it is important to me to have this conversation about fatphobia and attractiveness in a culturally specific context to explore the ways these issues present themselves differently from the mainstream Western norms. It is my long-term hope that we collectively dream about and build the capacity to honor all bodies in their ever-changing forms.

*Frances Ya-Chu Cowhig, Jacqueline Goldfinger,
Virginia Grise, Rachel Lynett, Neil Wechsler, and
Leah Nanako Winkler*

Special Thanks

Nkenna Akunna

Tatiana-Marie Carlo

Ina Chang

Myka Cue

Lisa D'Amour

Patrick Elizalde

Mario Gomez

Michael Hisamoto

Julia Jarcho

Melissa Kievman

Hyung Jin Lee

Alina Li

Christopher Lindsay

Aileen Wen McGroddy

Jenny Nguyen Nelson

Jules Pashall

Ro Reddick

Luis Ra Rivera

Sophia Skiles

Laura Stokes

Jesús I. Valles

Sarah Wansley

Robin Zeng

And everyone who gave me feedback and/or worked on the play.

Production History

Northern Stage New Works Now Festival Staged Reading 2022

Directed by Aileen Wen McGroddy

Cast

Ina Chang

Ariel Estrada

Sam Hamashima

Narea Kang

Zoë Kim

Christina Liang

Roger Yeh

Annie Yim

Brown University Writing is Live Festival Workshop
Production 2020

Directed by Tatiana-Marie Carlo

Cast

   Myka Cue

   Patrick Elizalde

   Michael Hisamoto

   Alina Li

   Christopher Lindsay

   Jenny Nguyen Nelson

   Luis Ra Rivera

   Robin Zeng

Jar of Fat

Cast

ABILENE   f, Korean, child to adult

CLEMENTINE   f, Korean, child to adult

MOM   f, Korean, 20s to 40s

DAD   m, Korean, 20s to 40s

LEO   m, Korean, adolescent to adult

CHRISTIAN   m, Korean, adolescent to adult

REVEREND   f, Korean, 40s to 50s

HALMUHNEE   f, Korean, a dead grandmother, not
                   physically seen but deeply felt

THE ASIAN ENSEMBLE

  FACE READER

  JAPANESE MILK TOAST

  WHOLE WHEAT TOAST

  RACCOON

  POSSUM

PSYCHIC HOTLINE OPERATOR

1-900-ANNOUNCER

PARISHIONERS

SCREAMING GIRLS

OLD DOLL

YOUNG DOLL

MOMMY SWAN

DADDY SWAN

CYGNETS

A NOTE ON CASTING AND PRODUCTIONS

Let's reclaim the word *fat* as a neutral descriptor, not an insult. It is my hope that fat actors, fat directors, and/or those who have experienced anti-fat bias are prioritized for casting and cared for in all productions. Please, no fat suits. The weight loss in the play should be depicted theatrically.

The play must be cast entirely with Asian and/or multi-racial/mixed Asian actors; some should have Korean language skills for pronunciation and intonation. If a production is cast with mixed Black-Asian actors, the production team should consider how anti-Black racism operates within our communities and take care not to cause harm. I am open to conversations about script changes that are related to acknowledging the reality of such racial dynamics.

A minimum of eight actors is needed; Asian Ensemble roles can be double cast. No actor is needed for HALMUHNEE.

Only Look at Beauty

At a park with a lake. DAD *kneels, holds an urn holding his mother,* HALMUHNEE [할머니]*, *and places it on a small table low to the ground for an ancestral ritual on a picnic blanket.* MOM *kneels beside* DAD *to assist him.*

DAD   *Umma* [엄마]** I am sorry I had to cremate you and that you live in such a humble vessel. But I promise you that I will make enough money to buy the family grave that will reunite us. Till then, here are your favorite Benson & Hedges smokes and a bottle of soju.

MOM *lights her a cigarette and pours her some soju. The couple bow to* HALMUHNEE. *Sounds of swans squawking.* MOM *sits and nuzzles against* DAD. *He hand feeds her pieces of* kimbap [김밥]†.

MOM   Hon, we are bringing two souls into the world that will make your *Uhmohnee* [어머니]‡ proud.

DAD   I hope they will be as beautiful and slender as you. Like those swans.

---

* Grandmother.

** Mom.

† Korean seaweed rice roll.

‡ Mother.

MOM   I love how swans look. It's breathtaking how long their necks are, and their feathery bodies look like white peonies floating on the lake. So elegant to have a white body with just a touch of tasteful eye makeup and a flash of orange beak. It's a beauty that's almost holy. But they are such spiteful bastards.

DAD   Well, just keep looking at them and let their beauty absorb into our twins' bloodstreams.

MOM   If you really wanted me to absorb their beauty, you could make me a swan pie. HA-HA.

DAD   Excuse me?

MOM   The Tudors would call them swan pie coffin. You simply defeather, parboil, season, and bake swan meat in a beautifully decorated pastry coffin.

DAD   Well, this kimbap will have to do. Open. Aaaah.

DAD *attempts to feed her the end of a kimbap roll. A swan squawking is heard.*

MOM   Are you feeding me the ugly, raggedy ends of the kimbap? What's wrong with you? You want our kids to turn out ugly? Beautiful food makes beautiful children. Feed me a perfect piece from the middle.

DAD   I'll be right back.

MOM   Where are you going?

DAD *exits. Sounds of intense confrontation and struggle. Angry and grieving swan squawking is heard.*

MOM   That sounded awful. What's going on?

DAD *reenters with a dead juvenile swan in his hand.*

MOM   *Yobo* [여보]*. What did you do? Don't you know swans are violently beautiful creatures?

DAD   I caught a swan to make a swan coffin for you. Or swan jerky. Or swan kimbap! You can eat it to make our girls very beautiful.

Swan squawking intensifies. Sounds of massive swan wings flapping. They approach MOM *and* DAD.

MOM   Um. We should go before they rip our faces off. NOW!

Panicked, they exit with HALMUHNEE'S *urn.*

* A term spouses use for each other.

That's Gucci?

MOM *and* DAD *wear Korean sheet masks as they rock their twin baby girls.*

MOM   Girls, let me tell you my absolute favorite fairy tale. Ooh, you're getting heavy. Maybe it's time to put you on a diet! HA-HA. This is a story from Italy. Same place that Gucci comes from! Once there were two sisters who were very fat and ugly. They lived together in a small palace. One day, a really hot prince walked by and heard them singing and wanted to meet up and, um, hold hands. The sisters thought this was funny. The first sister went to meet the prince in a treehouse to hold hands at night so he couldn't see how fat and ugly she was.

DAD   They held hands all night long until morning, when the prince finally got to see the fat and ugly sister's face. He got so grossed out he pushed her out of the treehouse. And she got stuck in the branches. She cried all night until fairies came and cut her down. She woke up to find she was all skinny and beautiful. She went home to her sister, who said, "Whoa. What happened?" And the first sister said, "This is the real me, under all the ugly skin." And later she said, "I'm gonna find the prince and hold hands some more." The second sister said, "Please, don't leave me!" But she was gone. So the second sister went to a butcher and asked him to cut off her skin so she could be free too.

MOM   But instead of becoming beautiful, she exposed all her organs. She lived a little until dying. The first sister who became beautiful was now immortal, and she lived long past everyone she ever loved. The end.

The twins start crying in unison.

You Have to Love Me

Years later. ABILENE *and* CLEMENTINE, *elementary school age, play with their Barbies.*

ABILENE   So wonderful for you to come over for tea for my eleventh birthday.

CLEMENTINE   So lovely to be here.

ABILENE   How is your lover?

CLEMENTINE   Great. We just bought a Porsche. I think marriage is all but next.

ABILENE   Splendid. Care for a hot chocolate cookie?

CLEMENTINE   Smells divine. Thank you.

ABILENE   Oh, the tea is ready. Be right back.

ABILENE *exits with her doll.* CLEMENTINE*'s doll takes two cookies.* ABILENE*'s doll reenters with a teapot.*

ABILENE   Oh, there were two cookies. Did you take both?

CLEMENTINE   Yes, I thought they were both for me.

ABILENE   You didn't think to save one for me?

CLEMENTINE   I thought you had more than the two.

ABILENE   And you ate them before the tea?

CLEMENTINE   I just couldn't resist!

ABILENE   YAH! WHO EATS COOKIES WITHOUT TEA LIKE A BARBARIC *SSANGNOM* [쌍놈]*?

CLEMENTINE   WHO SERVES ONLY ONE COOKIE AT A TEA PARTY LIKE A DESPOT?

ABILENE   How do you have the energy to serve God when all you serve is YOURSELF?

CLEMENTINE   You're just a stingy bitch, and this is, like, the worst tea party I've ever been to.

ABILENE   Your gluttony and selfishness are BLASPHE-MOUS to God.

Ominous lights and sounds.

CLEMENTINE   I didn't know this was a test.

ABILENE   You never know when God will test you. So you should always be perfect.

ABILENE *pulls out a bottle of discount holy water.*

CLEMENTINE   Please, I repent! I repent!

---

* A derogatory term for a male peasant, but mostly used in the modern context to mean a disrespectful man.

ABILENE   The time for repentance is over! Now for your punishment. I'll extract pleasure from watching your skin burn into vapors with this discount holy water!

CLEMENTINE   Please, give me another chance!

ABILENE   You're only sorry you got caught!

ABILENE *pours the discount holy water onto* CLEMENTINE*'s doll. They both make hissing noises. The doll screams in agony. Vapors rise from the doll's body as it falls.*

ABILENE   That's what you get. Ahh, serving God is so fun.

ABILENE*'s doll gets comfortable and sits down. Slowly,* CLEMENTINE*'s doll rises from the dead.*

CLEMENTINE   And what of you? You are Vain! Insolent! Spending more time at your makeup table than at the hallowed pews of church! Satan stuck his forked tongue in your ear, and now you can only hear EVIL.

ABILENE   No, I just wanted to look lovely for God!

CLEMENTINE   SCOFF! You think of catching the eyes of everyone BUT God. Spending all your money on plastic surgery so you have nothing left to tithe. You are sentenced to be burned on the hot coals of this Korean BBQ grill!

ABILENE   I promise I won't try to look good anymore!

CLEMENTINE   TOO LATE, DEMON! NOW, ENTER THE DEVIL'S ASHTRAY!

CLEMENTINE *'s doll ties up* ABILENE *'s doll, places it on a small Korean BBQ grill and turns it on. Sound of flames and crackling.* ABILENE *'s doll screams in agony.*

MOM (*offstage*)   Girls! What is that burning smell?

ABILENE   Shit! She's home!

CLEMENTINE   We microwaved bacon.

MOM (*offstage*)   Uh-oh. Too much bacon makes you fat, girls.

CLEMENTINE   Oh, we're just chewing it in our mouths for the flavor, but we aren't swallowing it. Don't worry.

MOM (*offstage*)   Okay, but not too much. You might accidentally swallow some fat. All right?

CLEMENTINE   Yes, Mom.

(*To* ABILENE.)

If she finds out, I'm going to tell her that this was your idea.

ABILENE   You can't snitch; you have to love me.

CLEMENTINE   Why do I HAVE to love you?

ABILENE   Cuz we ate and shat in the same place for nine months.

CLEMENTINE   No, I choose to love you. Love is a choice.

ABILENE   But so is betrayal. And love is not betrayal.

CLEMENTINE   Wait, what?

ABILENE   See, love is confusing.

Dad at the Grave

DAD *measures the family grave, which is just a large pit barely big enough to fit a few adults. He has cardboard cut-outs of each member of their family in their ideal size. He places them gently in the grave. He then takes them out. The twins enter and, facing him, make a large heart by arching their hands over their heads.*

DAD   Aw, adorable. Okay, now a little smaller.

They each cup one hand to one cheek into a C-shape as they puff out the opposite cheek to create a heart shape with their faces.

DAD   Cute. Very cute. Now just a smidge more wee.

They use their fingers to create a heart shape in front of their chests.

DAD   Just lovely as can be. Good. But daintier still!

They use their fingers to create a tiny Korean-style finger heart with their index fingers and thumbs. He sighs in approval. They all hug. He then traces their body outlines on a giant piece of butcher's paper as he tells a fairy tale.

DAD   Once upon a time, there was a *Gumiho* [구미호], which is a fox spirit with nine tails who roamed in the forests. One day she went into a village to smell some

delicious foods, when she saw the most beautiful man.
She fell in love with him at first sight, but sadly he was
repulsed by her fox form. In fear, he threw his shoe at her.
Traumatized, she went to a *mudang* [무당]* for advice,
and he told her she could change her shape into a beautiful woman if she ate a thousand human livers.

ABILENE   Eww! I hate liver!

CLEMENTINE   Dark stuff. I love Korean culture.

DAD   In a hundred days, she ate 999 livers and only
had one left to go. She went into town and broke into the
nicest house in the village and tore a sleeping man's liver
out of his body. As soon as she finished eating the liver,
her fox fur fell away and she emerged as a beautiful young
woman. But to her horror, in the morning light she real-
ized that the thousandth liver came from the only man she
had ever loved. The end.

ABILENE   Okay, Dad. We're twelve now, so we don't
need these baby stories anymore.

DAD   Sure. You are almost the size of grown women.
See this? This is how big you should be when you are fully
grown. Not much more. Maybe a trifle less. Okay??

DAD *holds up the ideal size cardboard cutouts to the girls'
actual outlines made of butcher's paper which are slightly
larger than the ideal size. Smoke from* HALMUHNEE*'s urn
snakes out.*

* Korean shaman.

Talking to Halmuhnee

ABILENE *and* CLEMENTINE, *now thirteen, regard* HAL-
MUHNEE*'s urn.*

ABILENE   You talk to her.

CLEMENTINE   Why do I have to talk to her?

ABILENE   Just you do it. I'm the eldest!

CLEMENTINE   By, like, an hour! We're both thirteen.

(*Beat.*)

Fine, you chicken shit. *Ahn-nyung-hah-sae-yo* [안녕
하세요]*, *Halmuhnee.* It's your grandchild. We've never
really talked, so we just wanted to say, "Hey, what's up?"
We heard you could, like, see the future from the grave.

ABILENE   Can you tell us our futures?

CLEMENTINE   What's it like to not worry about
housing costs anymore?

ABILENE   So do we, like, wait?

CLEMENTINE *listens to the urn.*

---

* Hello, grandmother.

CLEMENTINE   She says, "Get me some Benson & Hedges smokes, and I'll tell you everything I can see from here."

CLEMENTINE *opens the urn and gets ready to stick her hand in when—*

ABILENE   What the hell are you doing?

CLEMENTINE   She said to look inside her.

ABILENE   Look inside HALMUHNEE? Are you deranged?

CLEMENTINE *looks inside the urn. She sticks in her hand and pulls out a twenty-dollar bill.*

CLEMENTINE   She says, "Here's a twenty for your troubles."

ABILENE *starts screaming.* CLEMENTINE *takes her ash-covered hand to cover* ABILENE*'s mouth.*

ABILENE   Eww.

Being Rich Is, Like, Holy or Something

*At the Lamb of God Sunrise Halleluiah JESUS IS KING
Korean Church, which is located above a college prep tutor-
ing center and a Face Reader's business. REVEREND speaks
from the pulpit. The twins are now fourteen years old.*

REVEREND   When you give to the Lamb of God Sunrise Halleluiah JESUS IS KING Korean Church you are
building a bridge of faith to Heavenly Father. That is why
it is important for you to become rich in your soul, as well
as your bank account. Do not bury your wealth—it's an
opportunity. Work, be thin and nimble, so that you may
concentrate solely on building prosperity. Even the dead
show their success and failures by the size of their graves.
Therefore earn, earn, earn to build yourself a lavish vessel
towards God. And part of that vessel is your face and body.
Your face predicts your future. So parents, make sure you
get consultations on your children's faces to put them on
the right path. My dear friend the Face Reader will honor
a Lamb of God discount; just tell them I sent you. Now,
please, enjoy coffee time.

*Coffee time and mingling commence. REVEREND speaks with
FACE READER in a loud, performative manner. REVEREND's
sons, CHRISTIAN and LEO, stand by. Congregants act like
they aren't listening to them, but they totally are.*

REVEREND   See, that family over there made the largest
contribution to the church this month. Ever since the

father's promotion, they've been living large, you know,
for God. And I heard you upgraded your family grave.
Kudos.

FACE READER   Oh yes. I purchased the biggest grave
they had available in the best cemetery. Such luxury. We
even got a hot tub. We won't be able to use it, cuz, well,
we'll be deceased. But it'll look really nice inside.

REVEREND   Now, I want everyone to get on your level
one day. You've done WONDERS for these families. One
parishioner has already received seven marriage proposals
from seeing you just once.

CHRISTIAN and LEO   We feel sorry for the poor people
who can't afford to take their fat and ugly kids to you, Face
Reader.

FACE READER   Ugh, yes. How do poor people ever
live with their unfixed faces? How do they get jobs? And
find the right people to marry? You can't with faces like
that. Impossible.

(*Beat.*)

But boys, your arms . . . they're so . . . so weak . . . so
limpity-limp like soggy asparagus. You want arms to be
meaty, like a leg of mutton fit for a feudal lord. So you get,
you know—

FACE READER *mimes pumping iron while making gross
exertion noises.*

FACE READER   Meaty arms. Meaty life.
UNDERSTAND?

CHRISTIAN *and* LEO *nod their heads in shame.*

Ugly Hole

A little later. CHRISTIAN *and* LEO *approach* CLEMENTINE *and* ABILENE.

CHRISTIAN and LEO   Hey girls.

ABILENE   What do you want?

CHRISTIAN and LEO   You want to hang out?

ABILENE   That's nice to offer. Which seems unlike you.

LEO   We got a dude den in the church basement, and we wanna invite you. We got new video games.

CHRISTIAN   And porn. Have you ever seen porn?

ABILENE   Eww. We're at church, guys.

CHRISTIAN and LEO   Ha-ha. Just kidding.

CLEMENTINE   You got any croissants?

CHRISTIAN and LEO   Oh for sure.

CLEMENTINE   One day me and Abilene are going to open a patisserie specializing in laminated baked goods.

ABILENE   SHUT UP, CLEM.

CLEMENTINE   Just trying to speak our dreams into existence, Ab.

CHRISTIAN and LEO   Your Umma never lets you have a whole one, huh?

CLEMENTINE   We do get the crumbs of her affection.

The boys flirtingly hold the croissants up to CLEMENTINE *and* ABILENE.

ABILENE   For real, though. WHAT IS THIS? SOME KIND OF PSYCHOLOGICAL WAR GAME?

CHRISTIAN and LEO   We just like you. Yeah, like a lot. Let us start fresh. We just wanna do something sweet with you. So how about it?

They stand erotically close, almost kissing. The girls get flushed.

ABILENE   Look, the croissant, it's glowing! Glowing!

CLEMENTINE   You're hunger-hallucinating.

CHRISTIAN and LEO   You wanna have some fun or what?

CLEMENTINE   Won't hurt to check it out, right?

The boys lead them to a pantry closet. As soon as the girls are in, the boys lock the door.

CHRISTIAN and LEO   IN THE UGLY HOLE! UGLY HOLE! IN THE UGLY HOLE! WHERE UGLIES GO TO DIE!

CLEMENTINE and ABILENE   FUCK!

ABILENE   LET US OUT! YOU FUCKING YEAST
INFECTIONS!

CHRISTIAN and LEO   ENJOY YOUR CROISSANTS
YOU DUSTY UGLY FUCKS!

The boys laugh and run. The girls bang on the doors.

CLEMENTINE   Oh don't fret. We're going to get them
back good.

ABILENE   How? Should we kill them?

CLEMENTINE   What? No, dumbass. Steal from church.
BIG TIME. Take cash from the baskets as restitution. We
will get rich off our pain, Ab. RICH!

CHRISTIAN *and* LEO *dance to a K-pop number like assholes.*
Some other church girls scream oppah [오빠]* *excitedly*
offstage.

---

* Older brother. The term can also have a romantic connotation when a
woman calls her boyfriend *oppah*.

Read Their Faces, Predict Their Fortune

At FACE READER*'s office.* CLEMENTINE *and* ABILENE *poke their faces through two holes in a giant hanging white sheet that covers their bodies.* FACE READER *occasionally slurps noodles from an instant Shin ramen cup as they examine the twins' faces.*

MOM   So, please tell us everything.

FACE READER   Please be patient.

MOM   Patient? Ha! But we're Korean.

FACE READER   Did the Reverend say you'd get a discount?

MOM *nods.*

FACE READER   That's cuz she hopes to get a cut of every referral. And she is so fickle. One day I'm highly regarded, the next day I'm the tool of SAH-TAHN [사탄]*. Anyway, now please, *sssh*. I need some quiet to concentrate.

They slurp noodles loudly. The sound of stomachs growling from the twins is heard as they look at the instant noodles

* Korean pronunciation of *Satan*.

lustfully. FACE READER *uses a laser pointer to highlight and point at features of each of the girls' faces.*

FACE READER   So, your daughters, how old are they?

MOM   Fifteen.

FACE READER   Almost women. They have traditional Korean faces like big steamed buns, and they have slightly recessed chins. This means they can't be decisive.

MOM   That's okay. I can just tell them what to do.

FACE READER   Or you can get them corrective jaw surgery. Chin implants. Now this one.

MOM   Clementine.

FACE READER   Let's see your neck, Clementine. Her neck is nonexistent. Her head looks like an olive skewered on top of a sandwich. No neck whatsoever. Hm . . . this one . . .

MOM   Abilene.

FACE READER   Her cheeks are so sunken for being so chubby. This means she'll have money troubles if she marries the wrong person. I'd consider cheek implants or fillers. Their eyes are also too small. Like strings of fish poop across their faces. Too bad they don't have better *sangkkapeul* [쌍꺼풀]*, but that's an easy surgery. And

* Double eyelid fold.

they have no *aegyo-sal* [애교살]* under their eyes, so they look tired and withdrawn. Now their uneven lips predict unhappy love lives. Some lip injections should work just fine.

MOM (*panicked*)   Ha. But procedures are so, um, expensive! Can't you just crush some herbs and shit in a mortar and pestle and call it good like the olden days?

FACE READER   I could, but you and I know that won't really materially change your daughters' futures. *Aigo* [아이고]**, *Ajumma* [아줌마]†, you are such a natural beauty.

MOM   Oh, thank you. I try. I really try. I don't just wake up like this.

FACE READER   It's too bad your daughters didn't inherit your looks. They look nothing like you.

MOM   Surely my daughters can overcome their homeliness through hard work and virtue?

FACE READER   Nah. Ajumma, we're all going to suffer and die. Focus your resources on beautifying their lives. That's all you can control—by helping them reach safety in a dangerous world.

---

* Directly translates to "cute" and/or "charming" fat. Often used to mean eye bags that are considered attractive and are not discolored. It is a sought-out trait in Korea because it is thought to make the eyes look bigger and cheerier.

** A term of exclamation, like "oh my!"

† A term typically used to refer to a middle-aged woman. It can be used as an insult or as a sign of respect.

FACE READER *extends their hands for payment.* MOM *hands them an envelope.* FACE READER *looks at the amount and sighs.*

MOM *Jjom mahn duh kkakka joo sae yo* [좀만 더 깎아주세요]*.

FACE READER   This is not acceptable.

FACE READER *shakes their head sternly.* MOM *reluctantly hands them more money.*

FACE READER   Thank you. Here are my recommendations and the card of a plastic surgeon who does great work. Superb work. The best!

MOM   Okay, thank you so much. Very helpful. Let's go, girls. You can come out of your face holes now.

ABILENE   What were they talking about? Are we ugly?

CLEMENTINE   Did you just pay someone to tell us we're ugly?

* Please give us a little bit more of a discount.

Halmuhnee Says

The girls run to HALMUHNEE*'s urn excitedly. They wear Sweet Sixteen birthday hats.*

CLEMENTINE   Halmuhnee, we got you more of your favorite smokes!

CLEMENTINE *lights a cigarette and holds it up to the urn as if it were a face.*

CLEMENTINE   Please tell us our future, Halmuhnee.

CLEMENTINE *listens to the urn.*

CLEMENTINE   She says, "One will find endless beauty, the other freedom. Now I'm tired. Question time is over. Go away." Dang, Halmuhnee, okay. We'll let you rest. I'm gonna get the air freshener for the smoke. You coming?

ABILENE   In a sec.

CLEMENTINE *exits.*

ABILENE   Halmuhnee, will I become the beautiful one?

ABILENE *listens to the urn. She then gulps and sticks her hand in the urn. She pulls out a bloody swan feather and looks at it.*

ABILENE   I don't get it.

Sounds of violent swan squawking.

Interlude
Beauty Changes

OLD DOLL, *a nineties-era doll, stands in a conference room at a Doll Convention.* OLD DOLL *has enormous breasts, a tiny waist, and arms that are bent permanently at a 90-degree angle. Her head broke off a long time ago and is on the floor at her feet.* YOUNG DOLL, *a newer model, enters.* YOUNG DOLL's *proportions are "more realistic," with smaller breasts and wider hips and waistline. Her limbs are straight and make a crackling sound when they bend.*

YOUNG DOLL   Um, excuse me . . . can you tell me what room the workshop on "Salads and Feminism" is?

OLD DOLL (*speaking from her head on the floor*)   You made it! You're here. Welcome to "Salads and Femininity."

YOUNG DOLL   Um. I think there's some kind of mistake. I don't think this is for me.

OLD DOLL   We haven't even started the workshop yet, so how do you know it's not for you?

YOUNG DOLL (*muttering*)   Cuz your head is in the wrong place, bro.

OLD DOLL   What's that? I can't hear you so well from down here.

YOUNG DOLL   Uh, never mind. Thank you anyway.

OLD DOLL   Why don't you just stay for five minutes and then decide? Looks like you're my only participant, but no matter! Change starts with just one person at a time. So, Salads and Femininity—

YOUNG DOLL   I'm sorry. I can't do this.

OLD DOLL   What's wrong? Are you afraid of learning how to embrace the full spectrum of femininity? Trust me, it's not a linear process.

YOUNG DOLL   Okay, so . . . Um, sorry, I know we are supposed to respect our elders or whatever, but your kind of femininity is kind of like . . . really dated. Sorry. Like, it's not realistic to have . . . no head these days. I mean, you have a head but it's not, um, attached.

OLD DOLL   What I see before me is a hurt doll who judges before she plays.

YOUNG DOLL   And what I see is a set of tits and ass that were fashionable, like, a hundred years ago. Look, nobody wants what you have, okay? I'm the latest and greatest . . . okay? We are not the same.

OLD DOLL   EVERYBODY used to want a piece of me in their stories. And somebody almost did run off with my head. My Sally threw me off her balcony for an intense bungee-jumping storyline—and BOOP! My head popped off as I hit the pavement. I got downgraded to playing servant roles because no head, no story. Did I get depressed? Did I say, Poor me? NO! I got stronger. I believed my beauty got stronger. Every day I said to myself—

YOUNG DOLL   OMG . . . please don't. I can't. Literally gagging right now. DON'T FUCKING TELL ME TO

ACCEPT MYSELF JUST BECAUSE YOU OVERCAME
SOME INSANE HARDSHIP.

OLD DOLL   Oh, honey. It's okay.

YOUNG DOLL *sniffles.* OLD DOLL *pats her back.*

YOUNG DOLL   So your Sally used to take you bungee
jumping?

OLD DOLL   Yeah. I was in many spy intrigues with
high-speed Corvette chases, too.

YOUNG DOLL   Ugh. My Sally just makes me go to my
9-to-5 nonprofit job with no paid leave or health insurance.
I hate open floor plans, shitty coffee, and commuting.
Ugh! Is it because my boobs aren't inspiring? I want your
storylines.

OLD DOLL   How about we talk salads? Salads always
make me feel better.

Ugly in the Blood

MOM *walks over to* DAD *at the family grave. He is frantic. The grave is smaller, and he can no longer fit all the family cutouts in the grave.*

DAD   Yobo! YOBOOOOO!

MOM   What is it?

DAD   The grave is smaller. Why is the grave smaller?

MOM   Oh, is it?

DAD   AAAAAHHHH! The grave we could afford was already small. But not this small. Did I miscalculate? Oh, no . . . how will we all fit? I AM SUCH A FAILURE. UMMMMMMAA!

MOM   FINE. FIIIINE. I sold some inches off our grave plot so that I could pay our debts. And if we sold a little more, we could buy that diet swan powder that's all the rage. I'm told this will solve our problems and—

DAD   HOW COULD YOU DO THIS!? WHYYYYYYY?

MOM   For our girls and because beauty is priceless. One shouldn't be stingy about these things.

DAD   It's NOT WORTH a fortune.

MOM   I'm scared that their faces are in grave peril.

DAD   There are graver things we need to worry about than their faces.

MOM   Their faces will dictate their futures. I'm proof. If I didn't get beautiful, you never would have married me.

DAD   Darling, that's not true. What do you mean get beautiful? You've always been beautiful to me!

MOM   But you don't know! I used to be a plain girl, verging on homely, who was ignored and always forgotten. Until some swans ripped my face off at the park when I was eighteen years old. They found my nose in a ditch and my lips on a merry-go-round. But this was the best thing that ever happened to me because my parents paid for me to have plastic surgery. And when I got to choose my face, I became beautiful. Suddenly parking spots were plentiful, and everything was paid for me. My beauty is what caught your eye at first. People either ignore what's ugly or try to destroy it because it unsettles them. And it's my fault that they are homely; the ugliness is in my bloodline. That's why I want them to become beautiful, so they know its power. Now you know, do you hate me?

DAD   Darling, of course I still love you. All I care about is being together, in here.

MOM   I suppose I still love you too.

DAD   So you must stop fretting about me losing my love for you or our girls.

MOM   Promise?

They pinky promise Korean style, by wrapping their pinkies together and stamping their thumbs.

DAD   As long as we can all fit, we can be together.

Divination Cake

CLEMENTINE *and* ABILENE *wait for a cake to finish baking.*
A timer goes off. ABILENE *removes the cake from the oven*
with oven mitts. CLEMENTINE *has* HALMUHNEE*'s urn.*
ABILENE *pulls a charm out of her mouth from a bite of cake.*
It has a liver on it.

ABILENE   I got a liver charm. Look. It's glowing. What
does it mean?

CLEMENTINE *opens the urn and listens.*

CLEMENTINE   Halmuhnee says . . .

(*to* HALMUHNEE)

Neh, neh [네, 네]*.

ABILENE   WHAT? Hurry up.

CLEMENTINE   Liver, liver, liver . . . That you will
be . . . wait, what? I can't hear you. Oh . . . You will be
destroyed and reborn.

ABILENE   Cool, so I'll be, like, indestructible. Oh, and I
got a hand mirror too. Let me see!

---

* Yes, yes.

ABILENE *takes the urn and listens. She hears* HALMUHNEE
and smiles but quickly tries to hide her pleasure from
CLEMENTINE.

CLEMENTINE   Well? What does a hand mirror mean?
Are you going to tell me?

ABILENE   Oh. Um. A hand mirror means you'll get a
little bit pretty. It's not that bad if you eat it with tea.
Moistens the dryness of the crumb.

CLEMENTINE   Are you happy that you're going to be
a little bit pretty?

ABILENE *(lying)*   What? Nah. It's whatever.

CLEMENTINE   Oh, I got one. It's a toothbrush.

CLEMENTINE *listens to the urn.*

CLEMENTINE   She says an unfamiliar toothbrush
symbolizes betrayal.

ABILENE   Will it be you doing the betraying, or will
someone betray you?

DAD *(offstage)*   GIRLS. GIRLS. GIRLS.

ABILENE   FUCK! HURRY!

MOM *and* DAD *enter and smell the freshly baked cake.*

DAD   Oh girls, what in high gluten are you doing?

ABILENE   We baked a cake.

DAD   Oh, I see. Are you playing house?

CLEMENTINE   Oh Dad, we have body hair now. We don't do kid stuff like that anymore.

MOM   Oh, my girls are on the cusp of womanhood. But cake is very fattening.

DAD   Closer to adulthood means closer to death. HA-HA. Now, look girls. These are outlines of your bodies. Do they fit in the family grave or don't they?

DAD *holds up the paper outlines of the girls' bodies.*

ABILENE   Oh, we don't fit.

DAD   Are they good bodies? Or bad bodies?

CLEMENTINE   They're just bodies. Why do they have to be good or bad?

DAD   But when they don't fit in . . . and take up more space than we can afford, do you think that's good? Or bad?

ABILENE   Do you think our bodies are bad?

MOM   Well . . . I like your faces more now that you're done with hormonal puberty.

ABILENE   But do you think we have bad bodies?

DAD   Yes, we do. Especially if they're, you know, too . . . big . . . you know. Don't we?

MOM   . . . Yes.

ABILENE   Do you think a fat body is a bad body?

MOM   Yes, we do.

A chill goes through ABILENE.

ABILENE   I didn't know that.

DAD   Don't be heartbroken. It's not permanent if you just work at it. *Jjom cham-ah* [좀 참아]*. Deny yourself a little, and you won't know how happy you can be. We only say these things because we love you.

DAD *looks at them and then at the cake. They sadly throw the cake in the trash.*

* Just withstand it.

Reverend Promotes Dieting

At Lamb of God Sunrise Halleluiah JESUS IS KING Korean Church. REVEREND *feverishly delivers her sermon.*

REVEREND   Show some restraint. Keep the fat off your thighs so that there is more room on the pews for new parishioners of *Lamb of God Sunrise Halleluiah JESUS IS KING Korean Church!* Shame on those of you eating more than one danish at coffee time. Let this shame wash over you like warm icing and motivate you to do better. Now, in closing, dear congregation, I want to thank you again for your valued presence in our little church. You have made it what it is today. This is why the next thing I have to say is very difficult. At our last tithing, we asked you to dig deep in your pockets to help us renovate the church in time for *Chuseok* [추석]*. It has come to my attention that an individual donated a mere twenty dollars for this effort.

Shocked gasps from the crowd of parishioners.

REVEREND   Is Jesus only worth twenty dollars to you? HUH? I demand to know! Who dares throw a dirty twenty-dollar bill in Jesus's face? No name was put on the envelope, so I must ask you: WHO?! WHO!? WHO DOES NOT CARE TO HELP BUILD UP THIS CHURCH—JESUS'S HOME? WHO?

* A Korean thanksgiving holiday.

CROWD   *Uh-muh, uh-muh, uh-muh* [어머, 어머, 어머]*!

REVEREND   I don't have to tell you, my church con-
temporaries in the Republic of Korea all drive ONE-
HUNDRED-THOUSAND-DOLLAR European cars,
live in the most modern homes with servants, wear
custom-made suits made by expensive white-people
designers. And here, I live among you in a very humble
townhouse and drive my sons, Christian and Leo, around
in a Camry. And I shop at Ross.

CROWD (*murmuring*)   OH NO! HOW CAN IT BE?

REVEREND   Does God want me to represent Him in
this pitiful state? Have we finally reached the American
streets paved with the diamonds and gold promised to
us? Did we get colonized, bombed, and our countrymen
forever separated from their families so that we can drive
a CAMRY and clean our own toilets?

CROWD   NO! NO! NEVER!

REVEREND   Then I ask you, if you do not have the
courage to step forward, think twice, THREE TIMES
about what you donate today in the name of our Lord.
Your giving has been very light compared to years past,
dwindling each week. Remember, congregation, stinginess
is a tool of SAH-TAHN. Only God's love and grace can
bring your family fortune. JESUS! JESUS! JESUS is the
Answer! Baskets are coming around now. Thank you.

Baskets get passed around. CLEMENTINE *steals a wad of
money.*

* Oh my, oh my, oh my!

ABILENE   Mom, was it you who put in the twenty dollars?

CLEMENTINE   It was totally her.

MOM   SILENCE, YOU FOOLS. We're broke. Jesus is just going to have to wait.

REVEREND *makes her way around to mingle for coffee time.*

MOM   Girls, say hello to the Reverend.

ABILENE and CLEMENTINE   Hello to the Reverend.

MOM *lightly smacks both of them upside their heads.*

MOM   Oh my Jesus. Why don't you have any *noonchi* [눈치]?

ABILENE and CLEMENTINE   *Noonchi?*

MOM   The ability to accurately assess the social order in a room and act accordingly. GOD! WHAT BURDENS YOU HAVE BOTH TURNED OUT TO BE! For seventeen years you have been boulders crushing my neck. Now, make a good impression unless you want to die.

REVEREND   It's okay, girls. It's early, you're still waking up. Thank you for coming. Oh, how cute and plump they are. Only thing skinny about them is their cute little eyes, thin as embroidery thread. A pity they aren't as pretty as their Umma.

MOM   Oh, you're too kind, Reverend.

CLEMENTINE   Reverend, may I please help collect the
baskets?

REVEREND   Of course, darling. Thank you for offering.

CLEMENTINE *pockets more money from the collection baskets.*

Grave Practice

The family is at the grave with HALMUHNEE*'s urn.*

DAD   *Yeh deul ahh* [애들아]*! I have a present for you. Hope you like it. My secondary love language is gift giving! Now open, AAAH.

DAD *shoves swan jerky into the twins' mouths.*

ABILENE   What is this? It has the texture of despair.

CLEMENTINE   And the flavor of dried entrails. This is weaponized gifting, Dad. Not love.

DAD   It's swan jerky that I made myself. Been curing it for seventeen years. It will increase your metabolism.

MOM   And beautify your necks. Remember: Beautiful foods make beautiful bodies.

The girls take the swan jerky out of their mouths.

ABILENE   Swan jerky isn't pretty. I don't think it's gonna work.

DAD   What's important now is that we just need you to get a little smaller.

* Hey, kids!

44

CLEMENTINE   But we've literally tried every diet. The Sweet-Potato Diet.

ABILENE   Mediterranean diet.

CLEMENTINE   The Boiled-Egg-and-Black-Coffee Diet.

ABILENE   The Cabbage-Soup Diet.

CLEMENTINE   Paper-Cup Diet.

ABILENE   No-White-Foods Diet.

CLEMENTINE   I-U [아이유] Diet. One apple, two sweet potatoes, and one protein powder drink per day for five days to lose five kilos. YEAH, RIGHT!

ABILENE   Oh, and for two whole weeks we ate nothing but those tiny disgusting diet cookies that expand to the size of a walrus's fetus.

CLEMENTINE   And you get so bloated that you never want to eat again. Those gave me constipation, so nothing was coming in or out.

DAD (*robotic voice*)   I'm sorry, the mommy and daddy complaint line is now closed. Please call back during normal business hours. Thank you, good-bye.

(*Normal voice.*)

All right, girls. It's time to get into your new ride.

Everybody gets into the grave with HALMUHNEE*'s urn.*

DAD   Stop wiggling.

CLEMENTINE   We can't. We aren't sausages. And this isn't exactly comfortable.

MOM   Death isn't supposed to be comfortable or easy. So let's practice.

DAD   We're training you for death.

MOM   This is the grave you will be buried in, so you can get used to it.

CLEMENTINE   But it's so small. And cramped.

ABILENE   And we could still be growing.

DAD   Well, just don't get any bigger.

MOM   Maybe if you train your bones, they'll contort into the shape and size of the hole.

CLEMENTINE   My internal organs are turning into *paht jook* [팥죽]*. They're gonna start leaking out my ears, I swear. Okay, enough of this.

MOM AND DAD   NO NO NO.

The girls struggle out of the grave, sore and tired.

CLEMENTINE   I really hate you for doing this to us. Halmuhnee, can you please tell them we are going to be okay?

CLEMENTINE *listens to* HALMUHNEE*'s urn.*

---

* Red bean porridge.

DAD   What are you doing?!

CLEMENTINE   Halmuhnee talks to us, in messages from the grave. Maybe she'll calm you down.

ABILENE   What did she say?

CLEMENTINE   I don't hear anything. Halmuhnee. You there?

CLEMENTINE *opens the urn and gingerly puts her hand in.*

DAD   Get your hands out of my mother!

DAD *and* CLEMENTINE *struggle. The urn crashes and breaks.* HALMUHNEE*'s ashes scatter everywhere. They look at the mess, then at each other.* DAD *is devastated.*

DAD   UMMMA!!!!!! I can't even keep your ashes safe.

Everyone starts helping him scoop her up.

CLEMENTINE   I'm sorry, Dad.

ABILENE   She really did talk to us.

MOM   Girls! Stop it!

ABILENE   Please don't hate us.

DAD   I could never hate you. My life is unremarkable except for creating this family, which I love more than anything else. I killed everything else inside of me to make room for you. But I need your help now. Please keep us together, for me . . . for us?

They reluctantly nod. ABILENE *comforts him.*

Fuller Lips, Fuller Lives

Later that evening at home. MOM *approaches* ABILENE.

MOM   *Umma leul bwa* [엄마를 봐]*. Look at me.

ABILENE   What now?

MOM *stabs* ABILENE's *lips with a giant syringe.* ABILENE *screams.* CLEMENTINE *enters.*

CLEMENTINE   MOM! WHAT IS THIS?

MOM   It's a lip injection. Remember what the Face Reader said about your lips being uneven? And don't worry, I didn't spend any money; this is all just stuff I had lying around the house. It's DIY beauty!

CLEMENTINE   BUT WHY?

MOM   Think of it as a fun girls' trip to the spa, but at home.

ABILENE   I don't usually think of giant needles when we go to the spa. That's actually very stressful to look at.

MOM   Don't worry, it'll be fun. You girls are growing up, it's time you learned about upkeep.

* Look at mom.

ABILENE   Upkeep what?

CLEMENTINE   MOM! AB!

CLEMENTINE *holds up a container of cooking lard.*

ABILENE   YOU'RE USING COOKING LARD?

MOM   Yaah! You think you are Kylie Jenner? This is fine enough for you!

ABILENE   Mom, I feel weird.

CLEMENTINE   MOM! LOOK! SHE'S ACTUALLY PUFFING UP. AW, GROSS.

MOM   But I didn't even put in that much. Oh no, nonononono.

ABILENE *looks in the mirror.*

ABILENE   Oh my God. Now I am so much uglier than Clementine. Clem, I'm so ugly. So much uglier than you.

CLEMENTINE   It's really bad. Do something! DAAAAD!

DAD *runs in. He is confused and distressed.*

MOM   Oh no . . . Yobo, do you think cold cucumber slices will bring the swelling down?

CLEMENTINE   No, I think this is an allergic reaction or something.

DAD   Oh no. Abilene, are you okay? My poor baby girl!

MOM   I'm sorry! You told me to save money, so I—

DAD   I'm calling for help. Don't worry, girls!

ABILENE   I'm going to be so alone.

CLEMENTINE   I'm right here! Not going anywhere!

ABILENE   I'm going to be separated from the family as the ugliest one.

CLEMENTINE *snatches the syringe.*

MOM   CLEM! Give that back! What the hell are you doing?

CLEMENTINE *injects her own face and makes a guttural groan.*

CLEMENTINE   I told you, I'm not ever leaving you, Abilene.

ABILENE   You did that, for me?

CLEMENTINE   Yeah, dumbass. Duh. And shit, once we get so ugly, maybe everyone will leave us alone.

Ugly Togetherness

Lamb of God Sunrise Halleluiah JESUS IS KING Korean Church. CLEMENTINE *and* ABILENE*'s faces are wrapped in bandages. They unwrap their bandages. They look grotesque and bruised with sacks of fat hanging off their faces, remnants from the cooking-lard injections. They practice singing the hymn "I've Got Peace Like a River" in a church nook.* PARISHIONER *enters, sees them, screams, and exits while shouting for help.* REVEREND *enters, screams, and sprays discount holy water on them.* REVEREND *exits. The twins are at first shocked but then think this is hilarious. They continue to sing, more defiantly, with their heads held high.*

MOM (*offstage*)   PUT YOUR DAMN BANDAGES ON BEFORE YOU BECOME A NEWS STORY.

CLEMENTINE   But they itch!

ABILENE   We can't breathe with them on.

MOM (*offstage*)   DO YOU WANT TO DIE? DO YOU WANT TO DIE TODAY? NOW?

The girls tightly rewrap their bandages. They resume singing but more dejectedly.

CLEMENTINE and ABILENE (*singing*)

> I've got peace, love, and joy like a river
> I've got peace, love, and joy like a river
> I've got peace, love, and joy like a river
> In my soul
> Halleluiah! Halleluiah!

ABILENE   I am glad we are both the same degree of ugly.

CLEMENTINE   Same. Our comparable ugliness is such a comfort.

ABILENE   And because, well, we don't have to compare ourselves to one another—

CLEMENTINE   Since we are both equally ugly.

ABILENE   Like if you were all hotter than me, I'd still love you, but like I'd feel resentful.

CLEMENTINE   And if you were hotter than me . . . Why, I'd feel so lonesome.

ABILENE   And if you were hotter, you'd get hit on at the club, and I'd be left in the corner.

CLEMENTINE   At least we have each other. We can be ugly together.

ABILENE   Oh no!

CLEMENTINE   What?

ABILENE   It's only the handsomest monsters of Lamb of God Sunrise Halleluiah JESUS IS KING Korean Church and they're coming toward us.

CLEMENTINE   Ugh. The Reverend's sons. Maybe they'll be repulsed by our singing and leave us alone.

CLEMENTINE and ABILENE (*singing*)   "I've got faith like an ocean; I've got faith like an ocean . . . "

CHRISTIAN *and* LEO *enter holding a fundraising basket.*

CHRISTIAN and LEO   Hey girls.

ABILENE   UGH. Not you again.

CHRISTIAN and LEO   You got boobs yet?

CHRISTIAN *and* LEO *dance to another K-pop number like assholes. The twins scream at them.*

CHRISTIAN and LEO   Flabby Abby and Chubby Clementine, you want to buy some candy? We're fundraising for a band trip to Disney World. Jealous? Too bad they don't make the rides big enough for lard bucket piggies.

ABILENE   We don't need to buy candy; we already have some right here.

ABILENE *exposes an ankle.* CLEMENTINE *follows suit.* LEO *throws his shoe at them, which they dodge.*

CHRISTIAN and LEO   Eww, *moo da-lee* [무 다리]*!

CLEMENTINE   And boobs. We got those too.

ABILENE   You know you love it. That's why you're here, isn't it?

* "Radish legs," a derogatory term for thick calves.

CHRISTIAN and LEO   What? No. NASTY, NO WAY!

CLEMENTINE   But why can't you look away?

CHRISTIAN   Because . . . we've never seen anything like it.

ABILENE   You want to touch my fat ankle? Go ahead, Christian. Touch it.

CHRISTIAN *is conflicted. He wants to touch the ankle. He bends to try.* ABILENE *then knocks him over and holds him down while* CLEMENTINE *forcibly squirts Kewpie brand mayonnaise into his mouth.* LEO *is horrified.*

CLEMENTINE   SINCE YOU LOVE TALKING ABOUT MY LARD SO MUCH, HERE HAVE SOME! TAKE IT IN YOUR UGLY HOLE!

ABILENE (*to* LEO)   YOU WANT SOME TOO, YOU . . . YOU BULLY?

LEO *runs off in fear.* CLEMENTINE *takes the fundraising money.*

CLEMENTINE (*to* CHRISTIAN)   You say anything, you die.

The girls exit. CHRISTIAN *starts whimpering.* REVEREND *walks in.*

REVEREND   *Duhlohpkkae-weh-guhgee-noowuh-issuh* [더럽게 왜 거기 누워있어]*? AISSH. Get up.

---

* Why are you lying on the dirty ground?

CHRISTIAN   UMMA . . .

REVEREND   I cannot comfort you. Because God has
left us. Turns out making a living off Jesus is harder than
you'd expect. Fell on hard times and Jesus is not returning
my calls. Long story.

CHRISTIAN   What do you mean?

REVEREND   *Cham* [참]*. I raised you like little princes
your whole life. And now you will have to get the hands
of a laborer. Meaning you need to get your lazy asses some
jobs.

CHRISTIAN   We can't get jobs. What about all our
extracurricular activities? I got hockey, band, debate team,
robotics, mathletes, and all my other sports. We barely
have time to study. How are we supposed to get into
impressive colleges?

REVEREND   *Eeh-nom-ah* [이놈아]**, you'll be lucky if
you even get to college.

(*Beat.*)

Listen. Lamb of God Sunrise Halleluiah JESUS IS KING
Korean Church is no more. Our stingy churchgoers
stopped paying their share, so we haven't been making
rent. Been hurtling toward bankruptcy for a while. Oh
well, we tried, eh? So, you tell Leo that you both have to
quit all your sports and help me sell some Herbalife. Okay?
Now, help me pack up before the debt collectors come to
take our shit.

* Sound to express a bitter realization.

** You punk.

Good Fat

ABILENE and CLEMENTINE'S *faces have started to heal. They help each other remove the remnants of their facial fat injections.*

ABILENE   We have tried everything and it's never enough. I don't know what to do to make them happy.

CLEMENTINE   What if we just stopped stressing? There's good things about being fat and ugly too.

ABILENE   Like what?

CLEMENTINE   Don't you think being ugly has built up our character?

ABILENE   Who cares about character when no one wants you?

CLEMENTINE   I think our ugly made us more resourceful. And did you know there are good fats?

ABILENE   Yes. Fat in your lips, a little in the cheeks so you don't look old. On your ass, of course.

CLEMENTINE   But also the fat deep inside your—

ABILENE   Are you talking about subcutaneous fat on your lower abdomen? That kind is supposed to kill you.

CLEMENTINE   No, like the fat that keeps you warm.

ABILENE   But we have houndstooth coats for that very reason. Fashion and warmth.

CLEMENTINE   But there's fat that shields our organs. Gives us energy. Produces vital hormones. Fat that protects against trauma. Promise we'll be each other's FUPA against the world.

ABILENE   I promise.

CLEMENTINE   To formally ferment . . . no, foment our oath—take this knife. Slice your hand. And I'll slice my hand with my knife. And we'll shake on it.

CLEMENTINE *hands* ABILENE *a small knife in a sheath with a tassel attached to it. She takes another one out of her pocket.*

ABILENE   Don't you think we already share enough genetic material?

CLEMENTINE   Shut up. Don't belittle our blood oath.

ABILENE   But where did you get knives?

CLEMENTINE   They were passing them out at church when you were in the bathroom. They're mini-Korean knives from the olden times for women to kill themselves with before men can rape them, on a key chain.

ABILENE   Fine. But instead of killing ourselves we'll kill rapists.

CLEMENTINE   Duh, of course. Aren't they cute?

ABILENE   It's not that sharp.

CLEMENTINE   So we just have to stab pretty hard.
Okay, ready? One, two, three, stab! Cool. So listen, I've
been stealing from church for years now as restitution for
the bullying every Sunday. I saved up enough for an apartment deposit. Time to get out of the ugly hole of our
minds and into—

ABILENE   OMG. Are you talking about . . .

CLEMENTINE   MOVING OUT, BITCH!

ABILENE   But, like . . . that's like, wow. What will we do
when we move out?

CLEMENTINE   Whatever! Eat whatever we want. We'll
stop worrying about bringing shame to anyone but ourselves. It will be a dead zone for beauty. I'm going to glide
my enormous stomach from room to room looking for
another big stomach to touch mine at our palace.

ABILENE   But won't it be lonely?

CLEMENTINE   I don't need anybody but you, dummy.

Interlude
There's Always Someone Up the Ladder

POSSUM *and* RACCOON *hang out by some garbage cans late at night.*

RACCOON   I love the way you open garbage lids. You fling 'em open like doors to a mob-run casino.

POSSUM   Thanks. I like the way you do your eye makeup. Your whole face is cute.

RACCOON   Thanks. But I was born this way. So it's like waterproof. And damn, Lyme disease is scared of you, with you eating all the ticks in the city.

POSSUM   That's what I do. I find shit and eat it.

RACCOON   Hey, it was pretty ballsy of you to go after that frozen steak in the daytime. I woke up when you made that suburban human lady scream.

POSSUM   Oh, it was nothing. You're the lucky one.

RACCOON   Nothing? Come on! You grabbed that steak from her minivan so quick before she even had time to set her first load down. I wish I had the ovaries or testes to do something like that.

POSSUM   When you're hungry and afraid, you take risks.

RACCOON   I could never.

POSSUM   You mean you never have to. Never mind.
You're going to take it all wrong.

RACCOON   I can take it. Hit me.

POSSUM   Let's just go back to complimenting each
other.

RACCOON   But you only compliment my physical
appearance, whereas I have complimented you on the
multitude of your admirable animal proficiencies.

POSSUM   Cuz you don't have to have any . . .

RACCOON   EXCUSE ME? EXPLAIN YOURSELF.
I HAVE OTHER ATTRIBUTES.

POSSUM   Not really. You get everything cuz you got a
cute face and a bangin' tail. I mean, look at how thick that
tail is. I wish I had that thickness. Look at this shit. Is it a
bloodied tampon string in the garbage? Nope, it's just my
janky tail.

RACCOON   I still don't get what you mean. Why does
having a fluffy tail matter?

POSSUM   Like, you're hella fine, so you never have to
fight for food like I have to. You just get given food. Look,
I don't want your comfort or pity. I want your life.

RACCOON   Buddy, it's not that great. People try to
make you into a pet. Taxidermy you into a Davy Crockett
hat.

POSSUM   Oh to be immortalized BECAUSE OF YOUR BEAUTY. POOR YOU.

RACCOON   Yeah, so great to be skinned, salted, and glued on top of a plaster blob.

POSSUM   But you could have a nice life, sitting on a pedestal in the wood-paneled study of a rich neoliberal.

RACCOON   You're delusional, man. Rich people don't put raccoons in their studies. They like rapist ducks or stag heads and shit. Raccoons don't matter to people with offshore accounts.

POSSUM   Goddamn it. And here I thought I was just lower in the pecking order than you. I didn't know fucking DUCKS AND DEER factor into this. That's another stratum of beauty I didn't even consider. Might as well be dead.

RACCOON   Wake up! You're free to roam and eat all the garbage you want, unlike those stuffed fucks.

POSSUM   What do I have to aspire to now? How do I ever fill this emptiness?

RACCOON   Here, have some expired baloney.

Fat and Ugly Palace

CLEMENTINE *and* ABILENE *now live in their Fat and Ugly Palace apartment. Perhaps they have inflatable furniture and a landline telephone in the shape of a cheeseburger.* CLEMENTINE *handles a cabbage.*

CLEMENTINE (*mocking* MOM) "Girls, now is this a good vegetable or a bad vegetable? Remember, beautiful vegetables make beautiful people." Nailed it.

CLEMENTINE *takes a hammer to the head of cabbage.*

CLEMENTINE   BAD CABBAGE! BAD FUCKING CABBAGE!

ABILENE   Why are you hitting it like it hurt you or something?

CLEMENTINE   I vanquish all nutritious vegetables. We are free from their tyranny forevermore!

ABILENE   I kind of like cabbage.

CLEMENTINE   Fine. You can have cabbage. Only the kimchi kind, though. Here . . . now you do it.

CLEMENTINE *hands* ABILENE *a weight scale and the hammer.*

CLEMENTINE   Come on. This is a Fat and Ugly Palace tradition. We need to commemorate our one-year anniversary of living in freedom!

ABILENE *hits the scale with the hammer half-heartedly.*

CLEMENTINE   Harder! Remember all the times you had to stand on it, and it'd spit out offensive numbers at you?

ABILENE   Uh-huh. Bad scale. BAD FUCKING SCALE!

CLEMENTINE   HIT IT! HIT IT! HIT IT! THAT'S IT! *Aah-sah* [아싸]*!

ABILENE *pulls out a measuring tape.*

ABILENE   And remember this odious snake?!

(Mocking DAD.)

"Hey girls, let's see if you fit in the family grave today . . . especially after all that lasagna you had last night."

CLEMENTINE *lets out a guttural scream.*

ABILENE   What are you going to do to it, eh? Burn it? Rip it?

CLEMENTINE *shoves the whole tape measure in her mouth. But she can't quite swallow it. She gags and spits it out.*

CLEMENTINE   That was a mistake. Now what?

* Yay!

ABILENE   Let's ruin the blender! No more fiber and
prune smoothies.

CLEMENTINE   No. It makes milkshakes.

ABILENE   Right. Order a pizza?

CLEMENTINE   Let's do it!

CLEMENTINE and ABILENE

                    Fat and Ugly!
                    Fat and Ugly!
                    We are
                    Fat and Ugly!
                    Fat and Ugly!
                    We are
                    Truffles!
                    Ugly Truffles!

Dad Needs to See You

The phone rings at the Fat and Ugly Palace. DAD *is calling.*
An answering machine message plays.

CLEMENTINE and ABILENE   Hello, you've reached
the FAT and UGLY Palace. We're probably snorting
powdered sugar and eating Big Macs. Leave us a message
or donut. BEEEEP.

DAD   Hi, girls. I had a dream about you both. In the
dream, your Umma and I were already dead and buried.
You two were crying at our open grave when deep-fried
butter gushed from the grave's depths and swept you both
so, so far away from us. This is a bad omen. I know outside the protection of our watchful eyes, the world is just
your 24-hour all-you-can-eat-buffet. I get high blood
pressure thinking about you eating processed fried foods
and worst of all, white rice. You must stop consorting with
rice. Just tell rice: "You are poison, Rice." Any kind of carb
is the Antichrist, really. When I was a boy, we were too
poor to worry about what foods were good or bad for
me. I know you hate my nutritional nagging, but this is
my love language. Anyway, I've been worried sick since
you moved out. We miss you. BEEP.

CLEMENTINE   Cheer up. Stop caring. We're living
in our Fat and Ugly Palace, a happy place for happy
undesirables.

ABILENE   We've been free-range ugly, and I'm not happy. My left boob is still bigger than the other.

CLEMENTINE   And our generosity is bigger than our spite.

ABILENE   We have never been lusted after.

CLEMENTINE   But we have a decent vocabulary.

ABILENE   My pubic hair is more voluminous than my scalp.

CLEMENTINE   A full muff is good for the winter months!

ABILENE   My thighs rub together during the summer and look like skinned peaches.

CLEMENTINE   And no one can clean the meat off a chicken wing like you.

MOM *calls the girls. The answering message plays.*

CLEMENTINE and ABILENE   Hello, you've reached the FAT and UGLY Palace. We're probably snorting powdered sugar and eating Big Macs. Leave us a message or donut. BEEEEP.

MOM   Hi, girls. Your father won't let on, but he is going through the toughest time. He lost his job and our finances are in the toilet. He thinks he's a failure and you know how damaging such thoughts are to the blustery Korean male ego. Listen, girls, if you selfishly follow your dreams without regard to your ancestors, you're smearing shit on our family name. Anyway, it would really cheer him up if you came and had Korean BBQ with us. BEEP.

The girls look at each other. ABILENE *looks excited.* CLEMEN-
TINE *shakes her head.*

ABILENE   But Korean BBQ!

CLEMENTINE *shakes her head again and makes a throat-
slitting gesture.*

Interlude
A Toast to Beauty, Health Is Wealth

WHOLE WHEAT TOAST *and* JAPANESE MILK TOAST *hang out.*

WHOLE WHEAT TOAST   You're so fluffy. Luxuriously fluffy. Like a mattress for an NFL star. And your straight square lines are so pleasing to the eye. I can see where you begin and end—giving me serenity.

JAPANESE MILK TOAST   And you're so nutrition dense.

WHOLE WHEAT TOAST   Hard. Full of whole grains. That isn't sexy.

JAPANESE MILK TOAST   But you have such amazing pores.

WHOLE WHEAT TOAST   Potholes. I hate these scars.

JAPANESE MILK TOAST   Potholes that hold butter's pleasures.

WHOLE WHEAT TOAST   But butter wants to be with you. I've seen so many photos of you with butter. Sitting on top of you in rapture.

JAPANESE MILK TOAST   Sure, but do they really want to be in me? After photos, they just slide off me like a water

slide. You're wholesome nutrition. Look at those nuts.
Look at that fiber.

WHOLE WHEAT TOAST   But when people see you,
they see happiness, pleasure. They look at me and think
"lower cholesterol."

JAPANESE MILK TOAST   I'm not trying to minimize
your pain or say I have it worse. I don't need butter. And
butter in the end likes to be needed.

WHOLE WHEAT TOAST   You have so many lusting
after you: jam, Nutella, margarine. Aww sorry, I didn't
mean to say you'd be with margarine. Eww.

JAPANESE MILK TOAST   I've been with margarine.
Margarine was the most generous lover I ever had.

WHOLE WHEAT TOAST   What is margarine good for
except a quick rubbing? Wait. You degraded yourself with
margarine?

JAPANESE MILK TOAST   Aren't you being
judgmental?

WHOLE WHEAT TOAST   Why? Because I'm the type
of bread that helps you shit better?

JAPANESE MILK TOAST   As someone who has faced
derision for who they are.

Diet Powder

MOM *and* DAD *look at* ABILENE *stuffed into the family grave, which has gotten smaller.* DAD *cradles* HALMUHNEE, *who is now in a plastic freezer bag labeled "Halmuhnee" in black marker.*

ABILENE   This is not the Korean BBQ you promised me. I can't believe I fell for this subterfuge like a dumbass. I like hunger. It gives me something to look forward to. Eating.

DAD   Me too. Sometimes I miss wanting to eat so I buy a mound of croissants and dig my fingers into them deep, like I'm trying to fish a marble out of a crack in the floor. I keep waiting for something to bite my fingers off.

ABILENE   I can't stay in this position any longer. It's gonna cause nerve damage.

MOM   Well, yes. I see it must be harder since . . . well, the grave has gotten smaller.

DAD   Abilene. You never know when death will take us.

ABILENE   UGH. WILL THIS ASIAN GUILTING EVER END?

MOM   Not until we die. We're removing the obstacles to what you really want in life.

ABILENE   How do you know what I really want when you've never asked me?

MOM   Because I can already see you don't have it. Here. Take this diet powder made from crushed swan bones. TAKE IT.

ABILENE   Definitely not.

MOM   It's a miracle, Abilene. Magic. One tiny scoopful with your morning smoothie. You won't need much. Take it. Don't be afraid. Trust me. Take this. We sold everything to buy this small vial just for you.

ABILENE   What about Clementine?

MOM   Don't tell her. You know how butt hurt she can get. We only have enough for you, anyway.

ABILENE   But Clementine and I do everything together. We have no secrets.

MOM   And yet you came here without her. You know, this is for her own good too. Maybe it'll inspire her.

DAD   Our family graves are vessels of passage to our ancestors. Your mother, or, rather, WE decided to sell a huuuuuge chunk of the grave to pay for this diet powder. If you don't take it . . . and you stay looking like this . . . well . . . oh, the shame will follow us into the afterlife.

MOM   You don't want to be left behind, do you? You're the only one who can save our family from humiliation. You're special, Abilene. Make us proud. Unshame us.

They go to her and offer the powder. After a moment,
ABILENE *takes it.*

MOM   Good girl.

Transformation Begins

In her room, ABILENE *takes some of the diet powder. She then removes fat from her body, storing it in jars. She looks at herself in the mirror. She looks at the growing collection of jars of fat. At the same time,* CLEMENTINE *looks in the mirror in her room.*

CLEMENTINE   In here, no one's telling me,
"You're too bigly-jiggly-wiggly,"
that I'm a piggy and not a lil' twiggy.

ABILENE   You look better! Finer!
This is who you are really meant to be.
You are becoming the real you.

CLEMENTINE   No more nagging that I need to eat this
or not that.
Thought it'd be quieter in my head,
but now it's my own voice screaming:
"Ugly. Ugly. Ugly. You are Fugly."

ABILENE   A wisp, a hair, a whit, a driblet more
and you'll be so great.
Loneliness is a small price to pay
when you can fit, fit, fit
into a flyspeck or fleabite's dream.

CLEMENTINE   My chin still goes
oooooooooouopity-noop

instead of up and out, out, oooooooooout.
But why do I still care?
I think my thighs resent the shade of my stomach canopy.

ABILENE   Look at my stomach.
Wait, what stomach?
Oh, you mean this slab of solid granite.
Pow! Pow! Pow!

CLEMENTINE   I want to look better in pictures. In real
life. And in dreams.
But I HATE that I want that.
Sssh. Sssh. Ssssshhhhh.
Inside or outside my head, it's all the same.
Sssh. Sssh. Ssssshhhhh.
AB? *AAAAAB!*
I need you!

CLEMENTINE *approaches* ABILENE, *who scrambles to hide
her jars of fat.*

CLEMENTINE   Are you trying to lose weight?

ABILENE   What? NO.

CLEMENTINE   Then why do you have a tape measure
and a scale in your Amazon cart? We agreed—

ABILENE   Hey, my cart is private! STOP SNOOPING
IN MY CART.

CLEMENTINE   And why are you pooping so much?

ABILENE   Um . . . privacy . . . but I've had a bad
stomach bug, if you must know.

CLEMENTINE   We don't have secrets. When have we
ever had secrets?

ABILENE   Leave me alone.

CLEMENTINE   They got to you, didn't they?

ABILENE   No, will you relax?

CLEMENTINE   But you look fucking skinny. I can tell
even though you wear five bulky sweaters at once. You're
really trying.

ABILENE   I swear I am not!

CLEMENTINE   Have you forgotten our blood oath?
To never lose weight or get beautiful. The Fat and Ugly
Palace can only hold pleasure, happiness. No self-hatred.

ABILENE   Yeah, and it's been swell.

CLEMENTINE   You don't sound convinced. What's
wrong? Why are you hiding shit from me?

ABILENE   God, stop trying to get in my business all the
time. I'm just noting measurements for fun.

CLEMENTINE   Bullshit. You're trying to get skinny.

ABILENE   OF COURSE NOT.

CLEMENTINE   Oh yeah? Prove it.

CLEMENTINE *extends an apple fritter.*

ABILENE   Yeah, this is healthy.

CLEMENTINE   PROVE IT.

ABILENE *puts the whole apple fritter in her mouth.*

ABILENE   MMMMM.

CLEMENTINE   SWALLOW IT! SWALLOW IT ALL!

ABILENE *spits it out.*

Interlude
Hear-Me-Eat

1–900-ANNOUNCER   Craving something tasty but can't find it in your town? Your diet giving you the Restriction Blues? Developed a gluten allergy? IBS? Now, even if you can't eat it, you can still hear it. Call 1-900-EAR-MEAT to HEAR ME EAT! Each week we'll eat your favorite foods for your listening pleasure, right from the comfort of your recliner. BBQ pork belly.

Sound of pork belly being chewed.

1-900-ANNOUNCER   So much umami. So much wow. Crispy cheese dog.

Sound of a crispy cheese dog being bitten.

1-900-ANNOUNCER   Oooh, can you hear that cheese pull? *Ddukboki* [떡볶이]*.

Sound of ddukboki being chewed.

1-900-ANNOUNCER   *Jjol gyit, jjol gyit* [쫄깃쫄깃]**. *Jja jang myun* and *jjampong* [짜장면 and 짬뽕]†.

---

* Spicy rice cake dish.

** Onomatopoeia of chewy chewing sounds in Korean.

† Black bean noodle and spicy seafood noodle.

Sound of noodles slurping.

1-900-ANNOUNCER   *Aahh mah-sheet-dah* [아 맛있다]*
. . . Shame . . .

(Sound of Shame.)

1-900-ANNOUNCER   Regret . . .

(Sound of Regret.)

1-900-ANNOUNCER   Loneliness . . .

(Sound of Loneliness.)

1-900-ANNOUNCER   The crispiness is just so delec-
table. Now, just $2.99 per minute for the first five minutes.
So what are you waiting for!? Call 1-900-EAR-MEAT to
HEAR ME EAT NOW!

(Sounds of phones ringing and coins jangling.)

* Ah, it's delicious.

Reunion

At a supermarket. CHRISTIAN *shops.* ABILENE *enters.*

CHRISTIAN   Hey. Oh my god. Hey, Abby?

ABILENE   Oh. Hi.

CHRISTIAN   It's Christian. Remember? From Lamb of
God Sunrise Halleluiah JESUS IS KING Korean Church?

ABILENE   I go by Abilene. Only family gets to abbre-
viate it.

CHRISTIAN   Oh. Sorry. So sorry about my fuckup.

ABILENE   It's really not a big deal—

CHRISTIAN   Not a big deal? God, our names are our
identity. I just denied your identity.

ABILENE   I forgive you, I guess. So how have you
been?

CHRISTIAN   Honestly, shitty. Working through some
stuff. But I feel so much better now that I've seen you.
Blast from the past, yo. God, you look great.

ABILENE   Oh, yeah. I guess.

CHRISTIAN   Like, really great. You, like, look really different than when we were kids.

ABILENE   Thinner?

CHRISTIAN   Well—it looks like you've been taking care of yourself.

ABILENE (*lying*)   Actually, I got into a car accident and all my friends died in a fire. I got depressed and stopped eating solid foods for, like, a year. Which resulted in the beautiful weight loss you see before you.

CHRISTIAN   Oh, shit. My condolences.

ABILENE   Yeah, okay. Bye?

(*Beat.*)

CHRISTIAN   Do you want me to carry your basket?

ABILENE   Why?

CHRISTIAN   I don't know. I want to do nice things for you?

ABILENE   Really? You never did before. In fact, you made our lives a living hell. Your whole family did.

CHRISTIAN   You're right. I never had access to culturally competent therapy. I do now. Please let me be nice to you for once.

She hands him the basket and places a large frozen turkey in it. She adds a giant can of lard.

CHRISTIAN   Wait. Why are you walking so fast?

ABILENE   I hate the public.

CHRISTIAN   It's hard for me to keep up while carrying a 15-pound turkey. Can you slow down? So, listen. You want to go get a coffee or something?

ABILENE   So you can bully me in public? Hell no.

CHRISTIAN   God, I really traumatized you, huh? I truly am sorry. *Jincha, wahnjuhn* [진짜, 완전]*. Can you please let me make it up to you?

ABILENE   I don't know.

CHRISTIAN   You're such a beautiful person. I'm sorry I made you feel anything less.

ABILENE   WHAT THE HELL ARE YOU EVEN SAYING?

CHRISTIAN   That you're beautiful. B-E-A-U-T-I-

ABILENE *slaps him.* CHRISTIAN *drops the shopping basket. Then she gasps in horror, surprised at herself.*

ABILENE   It was reflex! I'm not used to you being like this.

CHRISTIAN   It's okay! I deserved it. So, about that coffee . . .

* Really, so much.

Skin Deep

CLEMENTINE *is on the phone with* PSYCHIC HOTLINE
OPERATOR.

PSYCHIC HOTLINE OPERATOR   Welcome to the
Mystical Cosmic Network. This call is $1.99 for the first
minute, and 99 cents for each additional minute, fifteen-
minute minimum. Who in this vast universe am I speaking
to this evening?

CLEMENTINE   Hi, my name is Cle—Carole. I'm calling
from Mountlake Terrace.

PSYCHIC HOTLINE OPERATOR   How's it going?

CLEMENTINE   Fine. I mean, not fine, obviously, that's
why I'm calling. Yeah.

PSYCHIC HOTLINE OPERATOR   Want to tell me
about it?

CLEMENTINE   I've just been feeling sort of blue. And
lonesome.

PSYCHIC HOTLINE OPERATOR   Can I ask how old
you are?

CLEMENTINE   I'd rather not say.

PSYCHIC HOTLINE OPERATOR   Listen, I can only help you with your woes if you trust me and the universe, Cle-Carole. So, what's manifesting for you, Cle-Carole?

CLEMENTINE   My parents don't get me. Like, they want me to change into something so bad, but I just disappoint them. And I just don't really have many friends, apart from my sister.

PSYCHIC HOTLINE OPERATOR   Well, some people don't even have that.

CLEMENTINE   Sure. But lately we've been having differences.

PSYCHIC HOTLINE OPERATOR   What kind of differences?

CLEMENTINE   She's acting so differently, like, in a way I haven't seen before. She's really into getting thin and beautiful. When we've always been ugly together. I think I just lost my best friend. I don't know what to do.

PSYCHIC HOTLINE OPERATOR   Poor Cle-Carole. Just write positive things about yourself on your mirror. If God's your thing, go to church. Volunteer. Charity makes you beautiful. And crying about the sorrows of the world is a great moisturizer.

CLEMENTINE   But . . . I don't want to do those things.

PSYCHIC HOTLINE OPERATOR   Don't let jealousy stop you from living your life.

CLEMENTINE   But I'm not jealous. I miss my sister. She's gone totally off the rails—

PSYCHIC HOTLINE OPERATOR   All I keep hearing is BUT BUT BUT BUT BUT BUT from you Cle-Carole. Very negative. You can't attract goodness and beauty if you keep BUT BUT BUT BUT BUT BUT-ing. Okay, so beauty in and of itself isn't that important to you. Beauty is in the eye of the beholder. And beauty is only skin deep.

CLEMENTINE   So, without my skin, I'd be free?

PSYCHIC HOTLINE OPERATOR   That's kind of a super-literal interpretation, Cle-Carole. Listen, why don't you try expressing how you feel to your sister?

Just the Way You Are

LEO *and* CHRISTIAN *pump iron in their apartment.*

LEO   Yo, what do you do think of my pecs? Swole, right?

CHRISTIAN   I don't know, bro. Can you make 'em dance?

LEO   Like a ballet.

(*Beat.*)

Bro, I've been having doubts about the dude in the sky
. . . Like, ever since the church went bankrupt, I've been lazy about my spirituality.

CHRISTIAN   Leo, I got you. We can find Him again together. Pray and shit. I had my doubts too. Like, God has given me everything I've asked for, smoking hot looks, a high-paying job, lots of sex . . . but in the back of my mind, I think that I don't really deserve it. Like, why am I so blessed? It's really not fair to unattractive, less successful people, you know? I've actually wondered, Is God dumb? Imperceptive? Unaware? But yo, when I saw Abilene again, it reminded me how strong my faith was as a child. And I really want to be, like, a good person, you know?

LEO   You sound like you're in love.

CHRISTIAN   What? Shut up, dude. Speaking of, now you need to get out cuz she's coming over soon. And I need to freshen up.

LEO *makes teasing kissing sounds as he exits.*

Later. ABILENE *and* CHRISTIAN *sit on the sofa together.*

CHRISTIAN   I noticed you didn't say grace before our candlelit dinner. You just pretended.

ABILENE   I stopped believing in Jesus when you and your brother locked us in the church closet. You bullied me into atheism.

CHRISTIAN   Damn, we were little shits. I'm sorry.

ABILENE   It's fine, it's whatever. What?

CHRISTIAN   You just look so beautiful.

ABILENE   Um. What about hot?

CHRISTIAN   Yes. So hot. So sexy.

ABILENE   Ugh, the male gaze is so . . . cringe. Fuck it.

ABILENE *kisses* CHRISTIAN *passionately, tongues are involved. Violins swell.* CHRISTIAN *pulls out a globule of fat from his mouth.*

CHRISTIAN   What the . . .

ABILENE   Oh shit, is that my fat? I've never had a diet work so well. Fat is literally melting off my body!

CHRISTIAN   AND INTO MY MOUTH.

ABILENE   This diet powder really fucking works. Would you look at that?

CHRISTIAN   But, um, I don't want you to lose too much weight. I like how you are, actually, and really whatever size you are.

ABILENE   HAHAHAHAHHAHAHAHAHHAHAHA-HAHAHAHHAHAHAHAHAHHAHAHAHAHAHA.

CHRISTIAN   Why are you laughing?

ABILENE   I'm sorry. It's just "I like how you are, actually, and really whatever size you are." Fucking HILARI-OUS, man. Um, can I have my fat back? It's like part of my set, my collezione*.

* Collection (Italian).

The Fracture

At MOM *and* DAD*'s house.* ABILENE *places globules of fat into jars that she hands to* DAD, *who puts them on the shelf. The shelf droops from the weight.* MOM *and* DAD *look at the growing display.*

MOM   Abilene. Oh my god. You look beautiful.

DAD   Like a mummified string bean! Right, Yobo?

ABILENE   Oh, thanks.

MOM   I knew you could do it. I knew it.

DAD   Look at my genes reaching their full potential!

MOM   OUR GENES.

ABILENE   Well, the diet powder you gave me really helped. I also drank lots of water. And kept my diet mainly organ meat and veggies. No carbs.

MOM   Incredible.

DAD   I'm so proud of you, Ab. You are going to get us all to fit in our grave.

ABILENE   Dad. If we didn't have to worry about fitting in there, what do you think we'd be worrying about instead? Or what do you think you'd be dreaming about? Dad. Are you okay?

A long pause.

DAD   Oh, but I stopped asking questions like that a long time ago. Who has the time?

CLEMENTINE *emerges from a hiding place, enraged.*

CLEMENTINE   Aren't you going to compliment my weight loss?

Her family shrieks in surprise.

MOM   Weight loss? What weight loss?

ABILENE   Clem, did you follow me?

CLEMENTINE   I lost weight too. It's just that I gained it all back.

MOM   It's rather exhausting having to cheer you on for the smallest little thing. Abilene, you'll be such an inspiration to all the other fat people of the world. Including those in our family.

CLEMENTINE   What the fuck.

ABILENE   I know you're pissed. But I did it for—

CLEMENTINE   No, no, no. Don't you dare say it was for me.

DAD   Clementine. We've missed you. Why didn't you come sooner?

CLEMENTINE   To get away from all this damage!

(*To* ABILENE.)

So you've been taking diet powder? I knew it wasn't a stomach bug, you liar. How could you do this to me? We were supposed to do everything together.

ABILENE   Clem. I just. I just wanted to feel what it was like to look this way. And it's just as everyone says. It's wonderful. And feels powerful.

CLEMENTINE   Seriously? You betrayed me for a feeling? You guillotined my heart. Like, who are you? Did I ever know?

ABILENE   Maybe you should have paid closer attention. All I ever do is what YOU want. No more.

CLEMENTINE   . . .

Swan Liver

ABILENE sits on the floor at a small portable gas Korean BBQ grill, cooking some livers. There are dead swan bodies around her. She pours herself shots of soju as she grills the meat.

ABILENE   No one ever warns you about how being too beautiful is a liability. When you're ugly, people want to fix you or get rid of you. Or pretend you don't exist. But when you're beautiful, people admire you so much they'll claw at your clothes and even under your skin. They will rip thick slabs off your being and sell your residue for rock bottom. But now, as soon as they get that look in their eyes, that famished, greedy look, is the time I like to—

She holds up her knife. A swan walks by. ABILENE twists its neck, stabs it, and plucks its liver to cook on her grill.

ABILENE   Swan meat is good and all, but I'm ready to level up.

Bye, Leo

LEO *pumps iron early in the morning.* ABILENE *enters quietly.*

LEO   Abilene?

ABILENE *slinks out of the shadows with blood on her lips.*

ABILENE   Well, hello there, Leo.

LEO   Hey. Christian's not here right now. You know I'd have seen you sooner, but Christian's always like, "NAH MAN, it's too early in the 'ship! YOU CAN'T SEE HER YET!" Well, damn . . . Haven't seen you since our time at Lamb of God Sunrise Halleluiah JESUS IS KING Korean Church. Those were the days.

ABILENE   Happy times, was it? For you?

LEO   Yeah, yeah, actually. I felt like I had a sense of purpose, community, you know? But as I get older, I realize that we are pretty alone, and, like, community isn't promised to us? But dude, I was such an asshole when we were kids, huh? Yo, I'm sorry . . .

ABILENE   You're sorry?

LEO   Yeah. Like *mucho, mucho* regret, bro. I never said that, huh . . . But look, I want you to know that Christian

is just so happy being with you. And it makes me happy
that you make each other happy, you know?

ABILENE   Yeah. So happy.

ABILENE *notices* LEO*'s back, which is now glowing. She moves
toward him, mesmerized by the glow.*

ABILENE   This is like a sign, right? It's a sign. I'm
ascending.

LEO   Huh? What? Ascending how?

She pulls out her little knife on a keychain.

LEO   Cute knife. I can talk cutlery all day. What you got
there, full or partial tang? That's a real cute, girly knife you
got there. Probably not a full tang. That's okay, though.

ABILENE   Hmm. But the blood. Well, it can't be helped.

ABILENE *holds the knife to* LEO*'s throat. He screams.*

LEO   SORRY! SORRY! SORRY! SO SORRY!

The lights go out. Sounds of blood gushing.

ABILENE   Why am I so hungry still?

Blood Bath Ballet

ABILENE's *world becomes awash with blood as she sets out on a human-liver-eating spree. Bone fragments, human fat, torn muscle, arteries, and gristle hit the ground, forming a pulsating, bloodied monument at her feet.*

Bye, Christian

CHRISTIAN *serenades* ABILENE *with a romantic ballad or reads her poetry (that's in the public domain). She intermittently and surreptitiously takes more diet powder. He then looks at an old bloodstain on his floor and groans.*

CHRISTIAN   Ugh, I'm pissed at Leo cuz he left a huge-ass wine stain on the floor without cleaning it.

ABILENE   Maybe it's not wine. Maybe it's BLOOD! MAYBE HE'S DEAD? AHHAHAHAHAHAHAHAHA-HAHAHAHAHA. Just kidding. Where is he, by the way?

CHRISTIAN   He texted me saying he was going back-packing to "find himself," and that was, like, a month ago. Should I be worried I haven't heard from him since?

ABILENE   Um, maybe he doesn't have cell service? And he's just having a real good time?

ABILENE *stealthily pulls out* LEO*'s phone and texts.* CHRISTIAN*'s phone dings.*

CHRISTIAN   Speak of the devil. "Bro, I'm having a real good time here in nature and shit. Sorry I haven't texted back much. Iffy cell service. Don't worry bout me. I AM NOT DEAD HA-HA." Well, that's a relief.

ABILENE   Glad you feel at peace. So, what did you want
to talk to me about?

CHRISTIAN   Oh, I'm kind of nervous about saying it.
Okay . . . Here goes. I love you. In fact, I loved you the
moment I saw you again.

ABILENE   Um. Wow. We haven't dated that long.

CHRISTIAN   I know. But isn't it great to have this kind
of certainty from a man within a single financial quarter?

ABILENE   Are you serious?

CHRISTIAN   Yeah. I want you to stop sucking in your
stomach. Don't turn the light off when we make love.
Because I love seeing all that jiggles, if it's part of you. I
just love your face with or without chins. I just love you.

ABILENE   HAHAHAHAHAHAHAHAHHAAHHAHA-
HAHAHAHAHAHHAAHHAHAHA

CHRISTIAN   PLEASE stop. Stop laughing.

ABILENE   I'm sorry. HAHAHAHAHAHAHAHAH-
HAHAHAHAHAHA. "I just love you."

CHRISTIAN   It's true!

ABILENE   Okay, maybe since I've gotten skinny.

CHRISTIAN   I always liked you being a little *toe-ng
toe-ng* [통통]*. I was just afraid to declare preferences
that are outside the dominant society's acceptance before.

---

* Plump or chubby.

ABILENE   AHHAHAHAHAHA!

ABILENE *looks at* CHRISTIAN*'s back, which is now glowing.*

ABILENE   Whoa. Your back.

CHRISTIAN   Stop. You're tickling me.

ABILENE   But your back. It's glowing.

CHRISTIAN   What are you talking about? Hey! Can we just finish talking before you fondle me? I'm being emotionally vulnerable right now.

ABILENE   "As soon as she finished eating the liver, she emerged as a beautiful young woman." I'm gonna get it.

CHRISTIAN   You're saying really weird shit. What's going on, Ab?

ABILENE *knocks him to the floor. She extracts her knife and swiftly cuts* CHRISTIAN*'s skin where his liver would be. The wound emits a strong ray of light, sort of like the bat signal.*

ABILENE   Welcome to the ugly hole, Christian.

CHRISTIAN   OH MY GOD, ABILENE! WHAT THE FUCK?

CHRISTIAN *dies.* ABILENE *holds up his liver.*

ABILENE   It's gorgeous and so juicy. Bigger than your brother's.

ABILENE *bites the liver.* CLEMENTINE *bursts in.*

CLEMENTINE   ABILENE! You're seriously dating our
childhood torturer? You've literally stopped living at our
place for like a month. Have you just moved in here, with
him? Like, how low can you go?

CLEMENTINE *finally sees* ABILENE *crouched over* CHRIS-
TIAN*'s bloody body. She screams.*

CLEMENTINE   HOLY FUCK HOLYFUCKFUCK-
FUCKFUCK.

ABILENE   How did you find me? Oh, duh! I share my
phone location with you.

CLEMENTINE   NONONONONONONONONO-
NONONO.

ABILENE   Look at Christian's liver, Clem. It's the
ultimate paleo. Fresh organic meat. The Greeks believed
the liver is indestructible and the home of life, soul, and
intelligence. Want some? As you can see, there's plenty to
go around!

CLEMENTINE   Abilene . . . I don't want this. You
CAN'T want this! And if you do, I don't know you
anymore.

ABILENE   We're sisters. We need to be there for each
other, even when it's scary. You know how Koreans say
your liver is big when you are being bold and brave. Clem,
now is not the time for your liver to shrink to the size of a
bean. Okay? I love you. Where are you going?

CLEMENTINE *runs out screaming.* ABILENE *calls out to her.*

ABILENE   REMEMBER! You can't snitch; you have to
love me.

Back at the Lake

MOM *and* DAD *sit on the bench at the lake. A squawking swan swims to the edge. He comes closer to them.* MOM *removes a donut from her purse and throws a crumb to the swan. The swan approaches while hissing. More swans emerge from the lake until they become a mass of swirling white feathers, beaks, and legs encroaching upon* MOM *and* DAD, *who are surrounded, no longer visible. Suddenly the first swan leaps up and knocks* DAD *into the lake and pushes him deep underwater with his massive wings. He pushes until* DAD *emerges from the water no more.* MOM *screams, but* DAD *is gone. She grabs the neck of the killer swan, but he overpowers her. He pecks* MOM *to death, plucks out her eyeball, and flies off with it. Swan feathers erupt from the family grave.*

Cut off My Skin

CLEMENTINE *looks into a mirror. She produces her small Korean knife. She presses the blade onto her flesh to skin herself.*

CLEMENTINE   "So she went to a butcher and asked him to cut off her skin so she could be free too. But instead of becoming beautiful, she exposed all her organs. She lived a little before dying."

Suddenly, CLEMENTINE *hears the violent squawking from a bevy of swans flying overhead. She breaks free from her dark bewitchment and drops the knife.*

Lights out.

Interlude
Swan Melodrama

MOMMY SWAN *sits atop a lake at her nest with her sleeping cygnets.* DADDY SWAN *glides in, agitated but trying to appear calm.*

MOMMY SWAN   Where have you been?

DADDY SWAN   *SSSHH.* Foraging. I tried to find our cygnets some eel grass and bugs. But no such luck.

MOMMY SWAN   You were gone for a long time.

DADDY SWAN   Why can't you say, "What a great provider you are. Thank you," instead of the accusatory "You were gone for a long time"?

MOMMY SWAN   Nobody is giving me a trophy for herding our adorable burdens on my own for hours on end. You go foraging once for the kids without bringing back anything, and you still need a parade thrown in your honor.

DADDY SWAN   The pickings on the lake have been slim lately, you know that.

The CYGNETS *awake and start gliding toward their parents to cuddle them.*

MOMMY SWAN   You look too unkempt and ruffled for foraging. And your eyes beam shamelessness. What were you really doing?

DADDY SWAN   I-I—can we talk about this later?

MOMMY SWAN   Listen, I know it's our swan culture to mate for life. But if you want to explore an open relationship, I am for it. Been thinking things have been stale for a while, anyway.

DADDY SWAN   Wait, what? Stale?

MOMMY SWAN   I'd just prefer you be open with me about your wants and desires. Okay?

DADDY SWAN   I have NEVER stepped out on you. Ever.

MOMMY SWAN   Listen, it's not going to work if you keep lying to me.

DADDY SWAN   You really think things have gotten stale?

MOMMY SWAN   Babe, there's a reason why monogamy and monotony start out sounding the same. If you get a lover, I want one on the side too. Like a spicy condiment.

DADDY SWAN   I'm late because . . . I killed today.

The CYGNETS say, "Kill?"

DADDY SWAN   Some other humans saw what I did and started shooting at me. I flew off for a few hours until they left.

MOMMY SWAN Why didn't you say so instead of letting me say damaging things about our relationship?

DADDY SWAN I didn't want to say it in front of the kids, but you kept insisting.

MOMMY SWAN Whatever, they aren't going to understand what you're saying.

The CYGNETS *say, "Kill."*

DADDY SWAN I saw two humans sitting too close to our nest. I couldn't have them hurting you or our babies. So I went up to them to scare them off, when I suddenly recognized them. They are the fuckers who killed our first child together, those many years ago.

MOMMY SWAN YOU SAW THEM AGAIN? I HOPE THEY SUFFERED IN DEATH. I wish you had come and gotten me. I should have liked to peck their faces off myself.

DADDY SWAN There wasn't time. I couldn't let them get away again. I knocked one of them into the water and I basically sat on its face till it drowned. The other one grabbed my neck. So I ripped that one's face off and plucked its eyes out. Anyway, *bon appétit*, my love.

DADDY SWAN *rolls an eyeball toward her.*

MOMMY SWAN Oh, babe. I've never had eye before. And you have avenged us. I love you.

The CYGNETS *chirp, "Kill! Kill! Kill!" in a crescendoing chorus.*

Something Back

CLEMENTINE *carefully places* HALMUHNEE*'s ashes from the plastic freezer bag into a cookie jar.*

CLEMENTINE   *Halmuhnee.* Please talk to me.

CLEMENTINE *listens to the cookie jar. She exhales deeply and reaches inside the urn. She pulls out a plentiful succession of her favorite foods and objects: a croissant, a donut, and a jar of kimchi.*

CLEMENTINE   Thank you. I love you, too. I wish I could give you something back.

CLEMENTINE *hugs* HALMUHNEE *and listens to her speak. The cookie jar lights up.* CLEMENTINE *pulls out a picture of her family.*

CLEMENTINE   No, I won't. Can't.

The cookie jar violently convulses, tipping over. CLEMENTINE *catches it before it crashes.*

CLEMENTINE   Halmuhnee, please stop. Please stop. I can't keep obsessing about dying while I'm living. It hurts. Their bones never ask for forgiveness. And neither will Abilene in the flesh. Love doesn't cancel that out. Halmuhnee?

A beam of light emanates from the cookie jar. CLEMENTINE
touches the light with her hand.

CLEMENTINE   Okay. Halmuhnee. Okay. I'll go. I'll be
dead the way you want me to be. But first, I'm going to
stay alive any which way I want. You'll all just have to take
me as I am and will be.

Last Time

Years later. CLEMENTINE, *much older and near death, stands by the family grave carrying her parents' bones and* HALMUHNEE'*s cookie jar.* ABILENE *enters, still appearing young.*

ABILENE   I've missed you.

CLEMENTINE   I've missed the old you. The one that wasn't a bitch.

ABILENE   It's been decades, and this is the first time you've talked to me.

CLEMENTINE   I was pissed at you for a long while, but I figured I should see you before I kicked the bucket.

ABILENE   Whatcha got there?

CLEMENTINE   Mom and Dad. Well, their bones at least. The swans pecked everything else off. And since they're both just bones now, there's enough room for me to fit in the grave without losing weight. Halmuhnee's here too.

ABILENE   Mom's finally smaller than a size zero. Just like you always wanted, huh, Mom? I'm sorry that this is what our lives amounted to. What a cramped life we worked toward. How are you?

CLEMENTINE   Me? I'm content.

ABILENE   Why? You look fucking horrible.

CLEMENTINE   I lived and will die on my own terms. I got so old, but you didn't. You look amazing.

ABILENE   Eternal youth or whatever is overrated. So what else you been up to?

CLEMENTINE   Just living my life. And dying, duh. You know, after you started taking the diet powder, I was going to cut off all my skin, like the sister in the Italian fairy tale that Mom would tell us? I was so angry at you that I wanted to cut my jawbone off. That way, I'd never speak your name again. But I decided I wanted to keep living to spite you instead.

ABILENE   I'm glad you did. Looks like you had a full life. Did you end up staying in the Fat and Ugly Palace?

CLEMENTINE   Yeah, and it was fucking awesome. I think you would have liked it. How has it been being beautiful like you always wanted? I used to want revenge, but now, I truly hope you are happy.

ABILENE   For a while it was great; I had lots of friends and lovers. But sooner or later, I'd get the urge to kill them and eat their livers so I could stay looking like this. Which can get lonely, you know? Anyway, I should have said a long time ago, I'm sorry. But we can be together in the afterlife. I'm finally ready for a good rest now, too. Living this long has been exhausting.

CLEMENTINE   But you're still alive.

CLEMENTINE *gently lies down in the grave with the bones and the cookie jar.*

ABILENE   Yeah, so? I'd rather be with my dead family than alone with strangers. Halmuhnee, I'm sorry for not visiting sooner. But I'm glad to be reunited with you and the family again. Clem, move over. I want to go with you.

CLEMENTINE *listens to the cookie jar.*

CLEMENTINE   She says you can't stay.

ABILENE   But I want to.

CLEMENTINE   There isn't space for you, especially since you are alive.

ABILENE   But the problem is, no matter what I do, I can't seem to die. I tried to die so many times. But it's no use. See?

ABILENE *stabs herself a few times with her small Korean knife to no avail. She keeps living.*

CLEMENTINE   That's bananas.

The grave lights up. CLEMENTINE *listens to* HALMUHNEE *again.*

CLEMENTINE   Sorry, Abilene. Halmuhnee says, "Take care of yourself. Come visit us. We won't have a headstone, but they're turning this cemetery into a park, so we'll be under a cool playground slide. Love you."

The grave closes as ABILENE *watches. She is alone.*

END OF PLAY

A Note on the Fairy Tales

The story MOM tells in "That's Gucci?" is a retelling of a traditional fairy tale inspired by the version found in Carmen Maria Machado, "The Old Women Who Were Skinned," *Fairy Tale Review* 12 (2016): 120–24. https://doi.org/10.13110/fairtale revi.12.1.0120.

Inspiration for the fairy tale in "Dad at the Grave" was drawn from a variation of the traditional Korean Gumiho fairy tale. For more on this figure, see Charles La Shure, "Kumiho," *Pantheon* (April 21, 2001), https://pantheon.org/articles/k /kumiho.html.